Thank you to those that have helped me along the way. My appreciation will always be endless.

I am creatively inspired by the world around me.

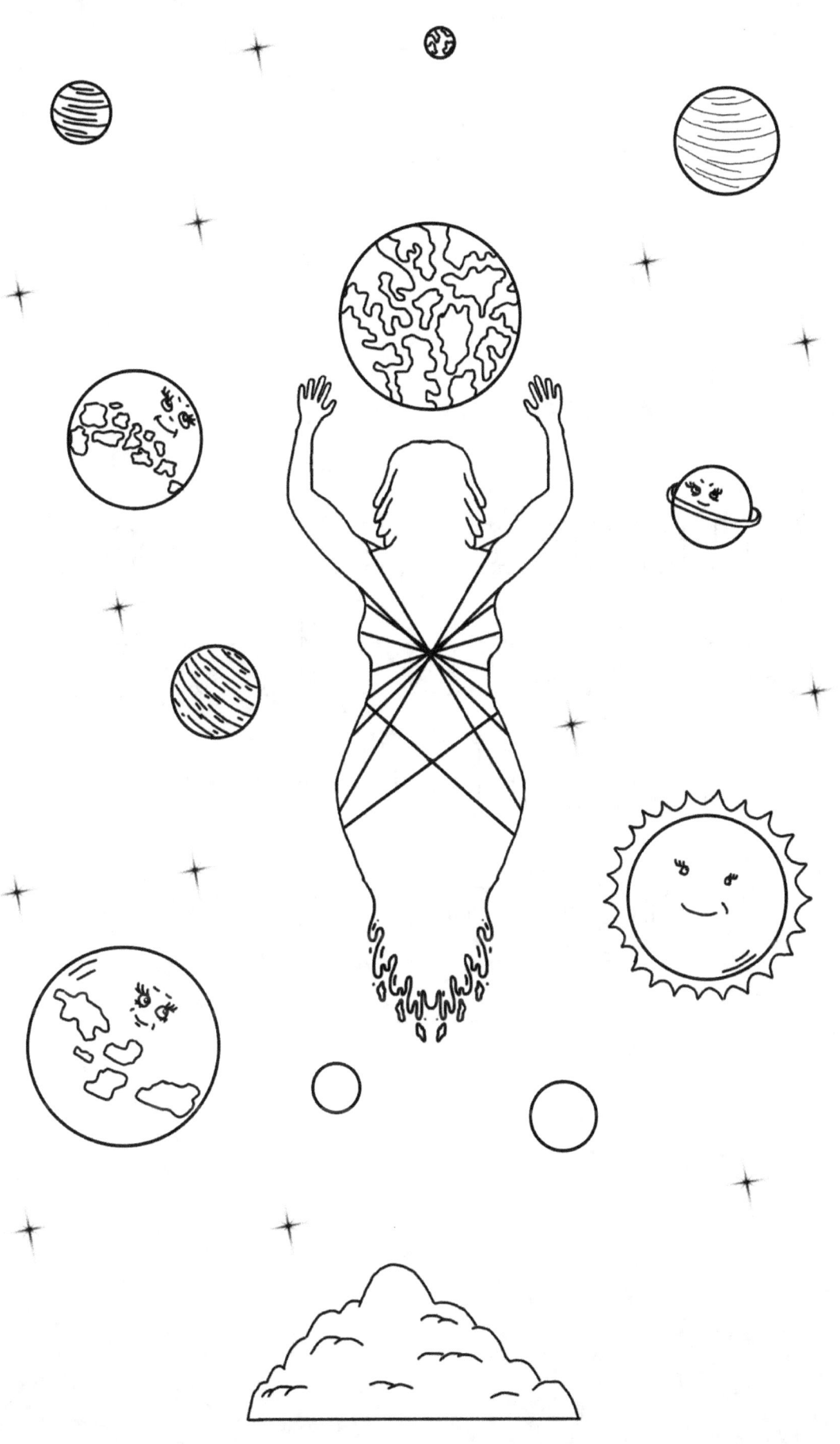

You have to give yourself credit for the days you made it when you thought you couldn't.

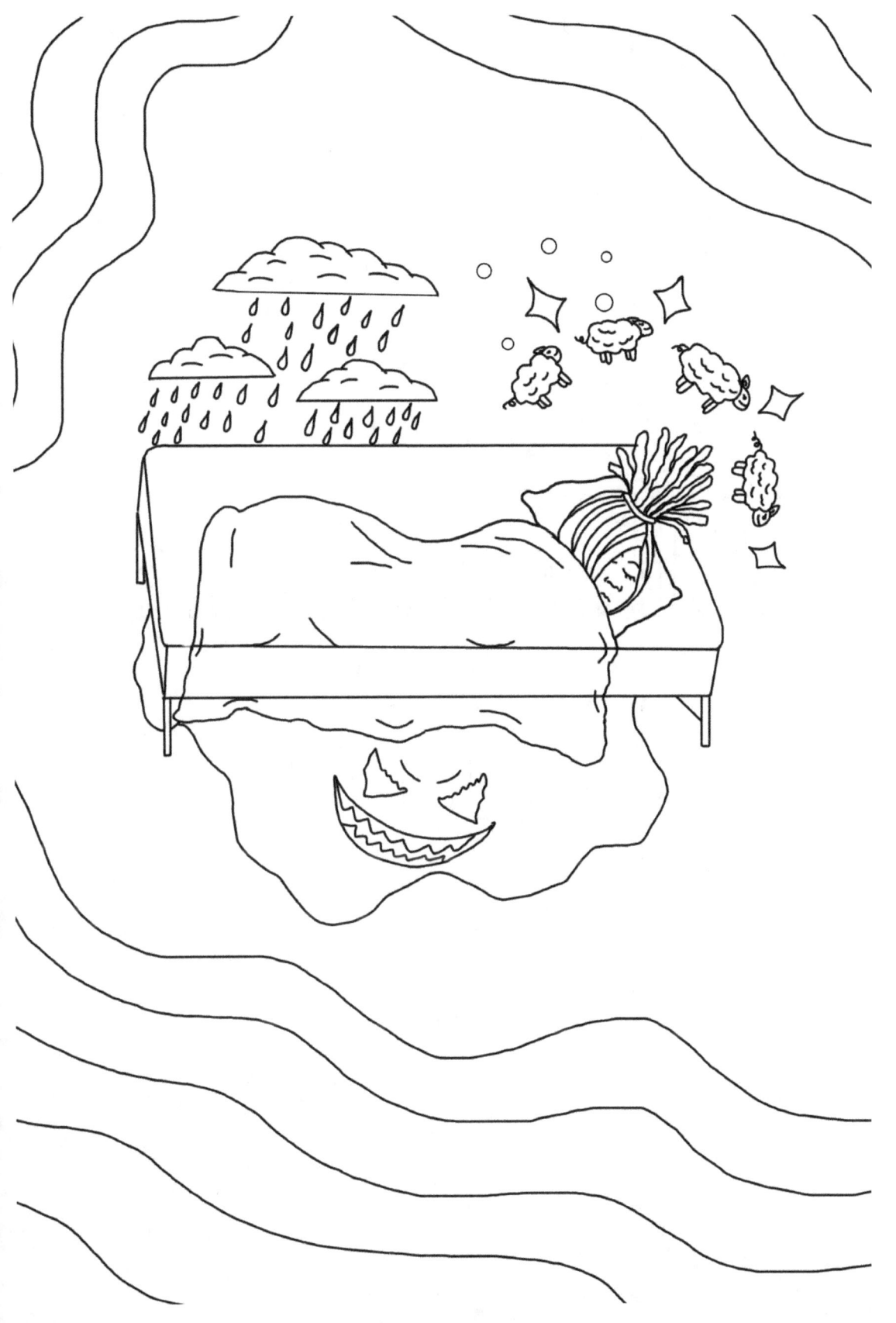

All bodies are beautiful.

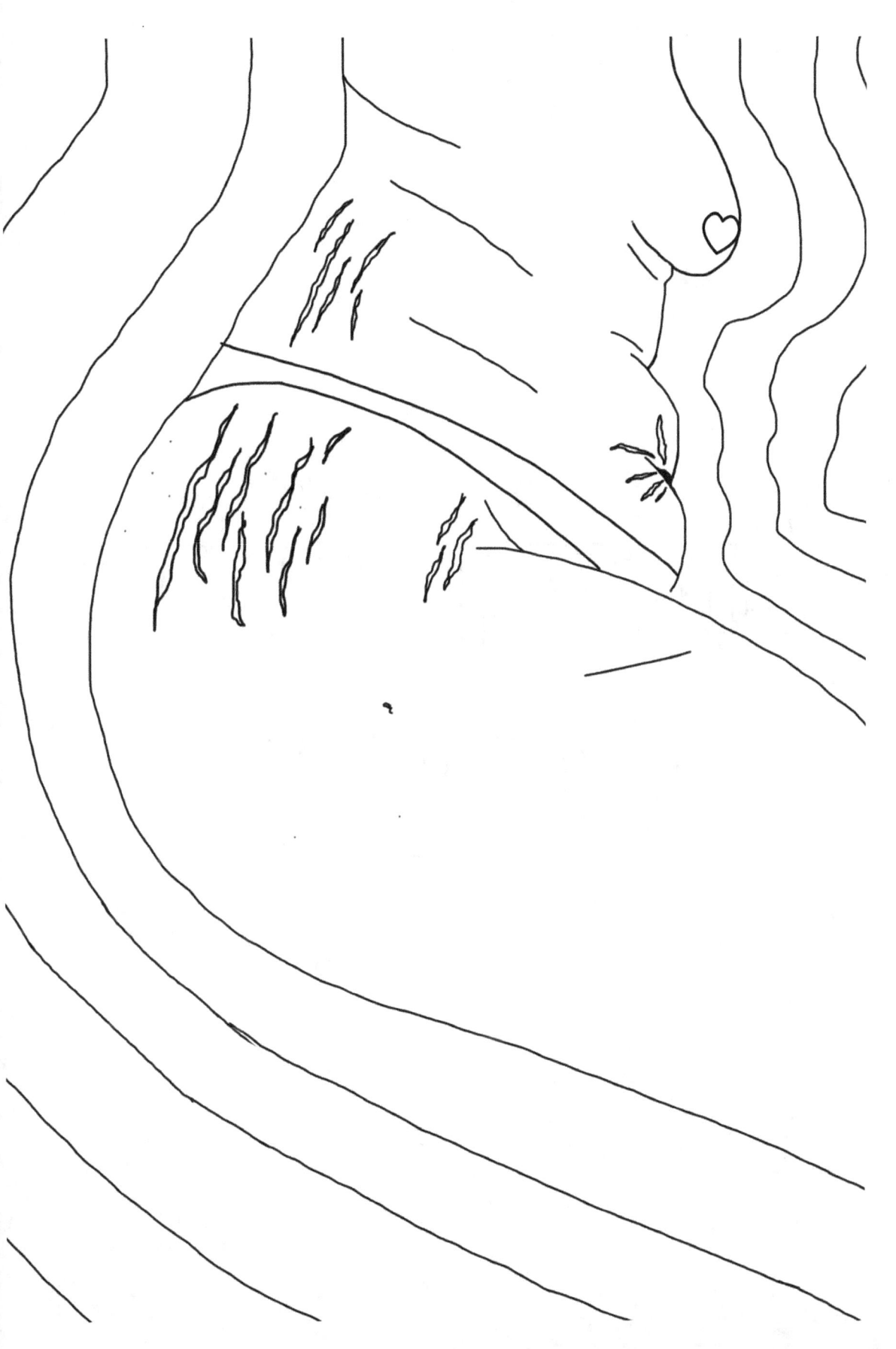

Grow positive thoughts.

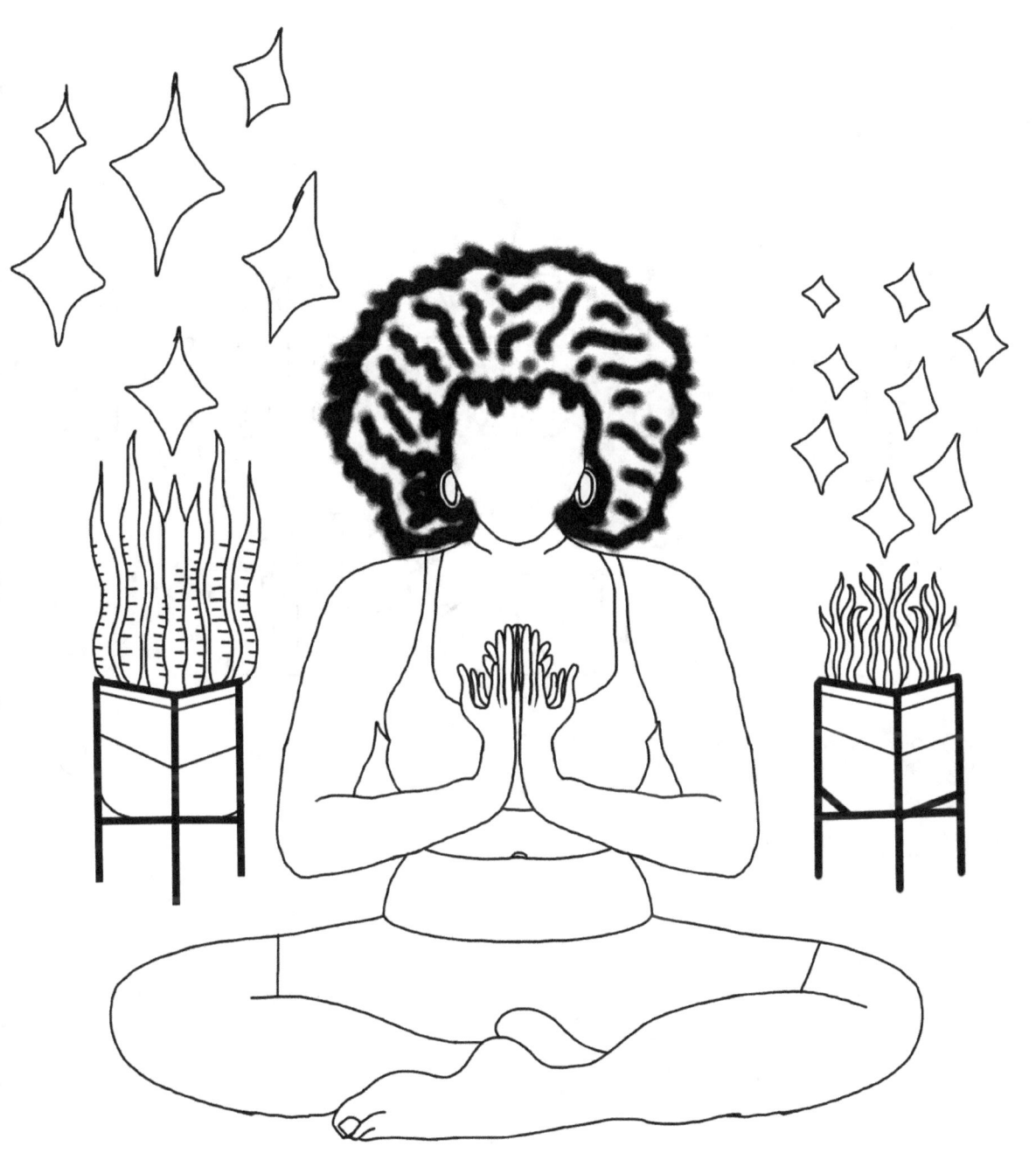

Speak kindly to yourself.

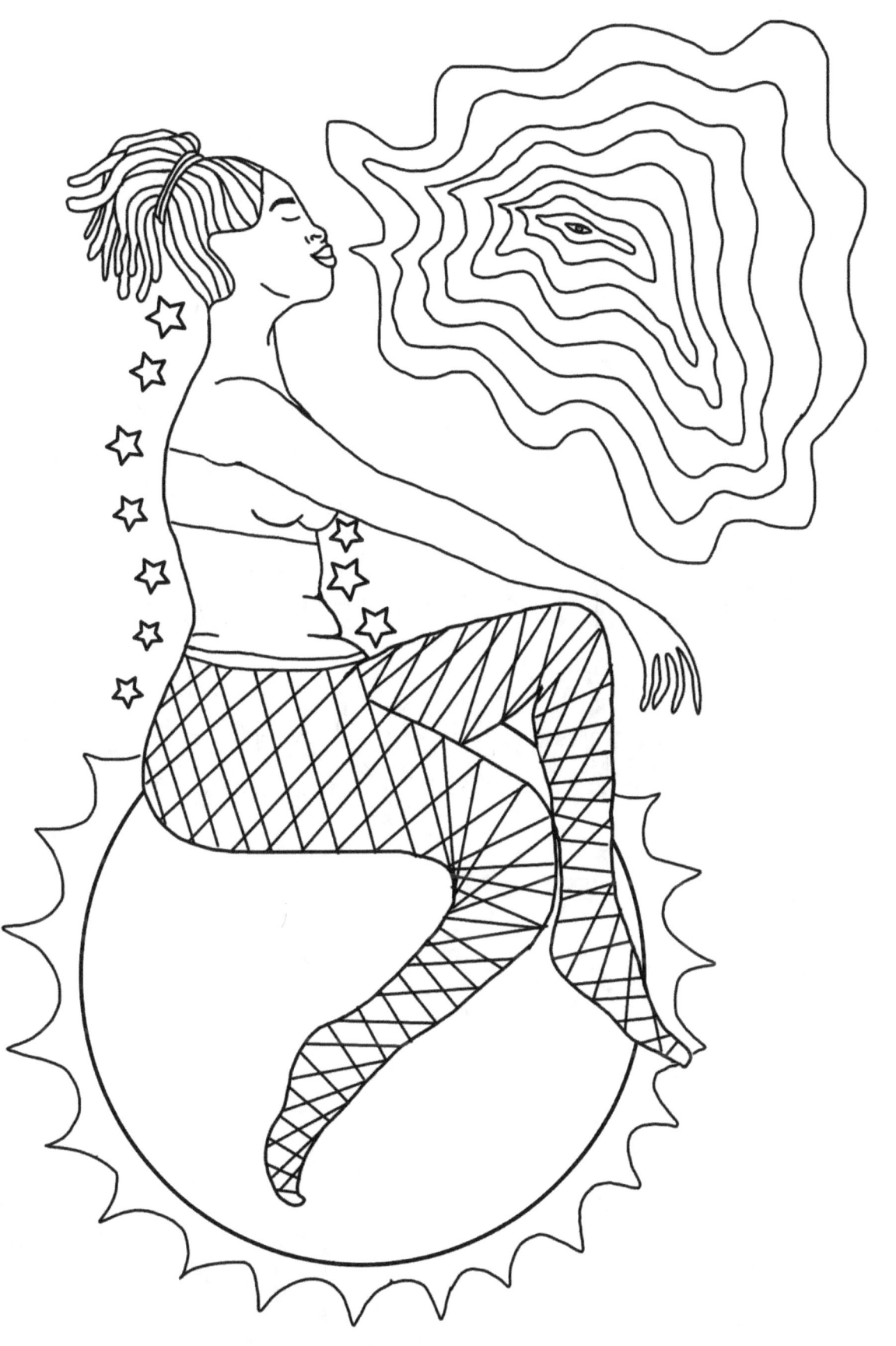

You are exactly where you need to be.

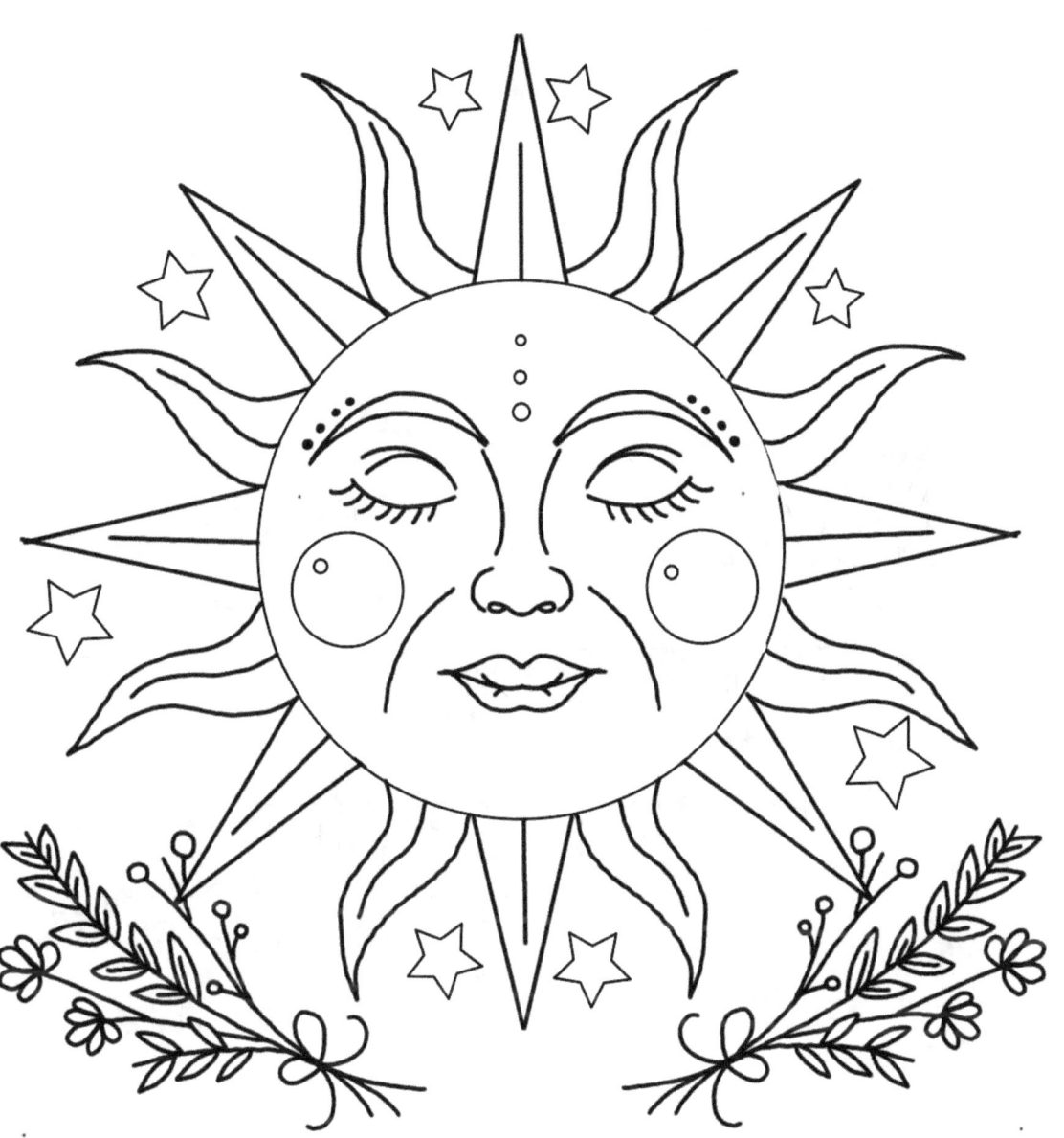

Never compromise your sense of individuality.

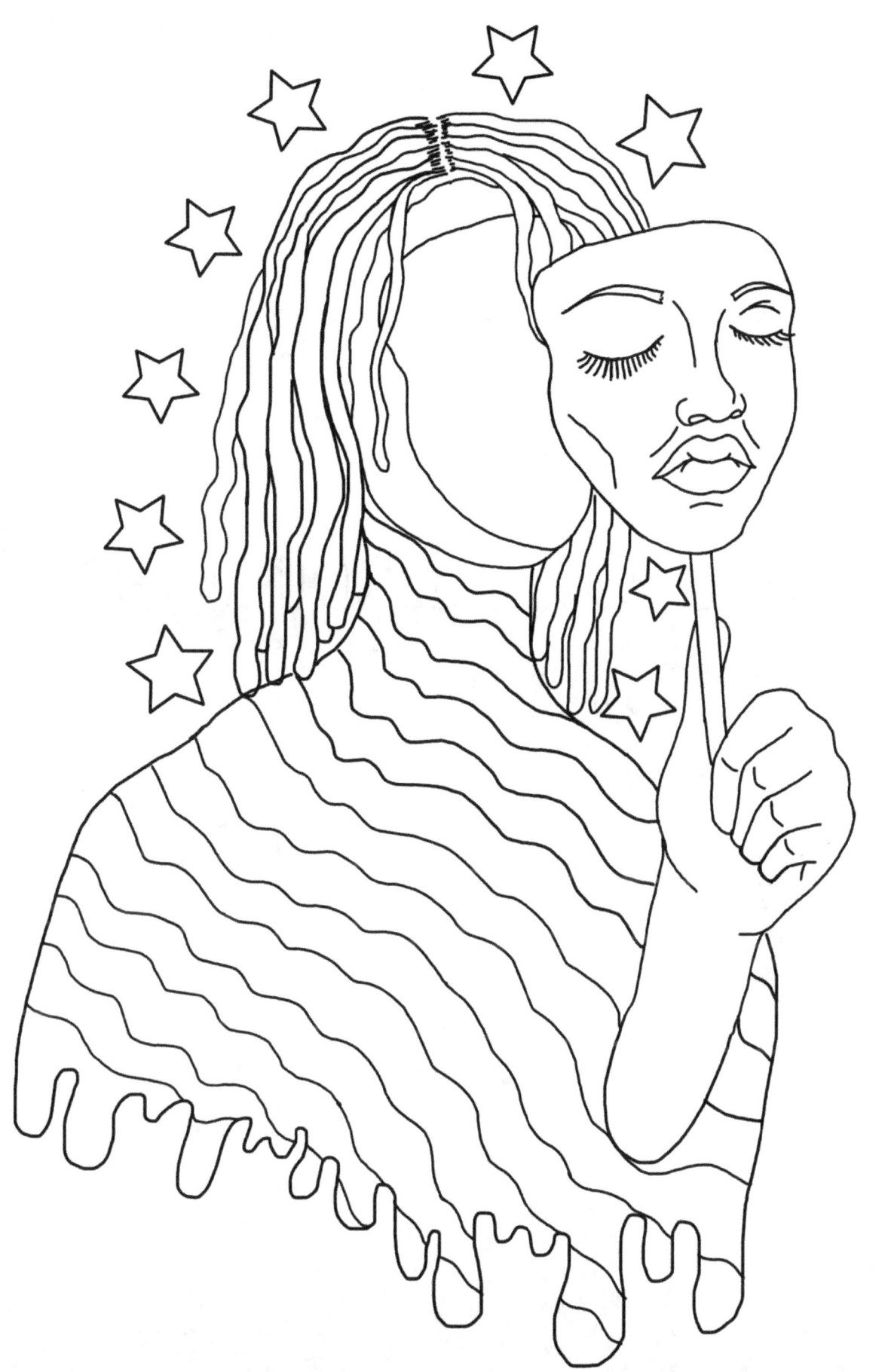

I am stronger than this emotion.

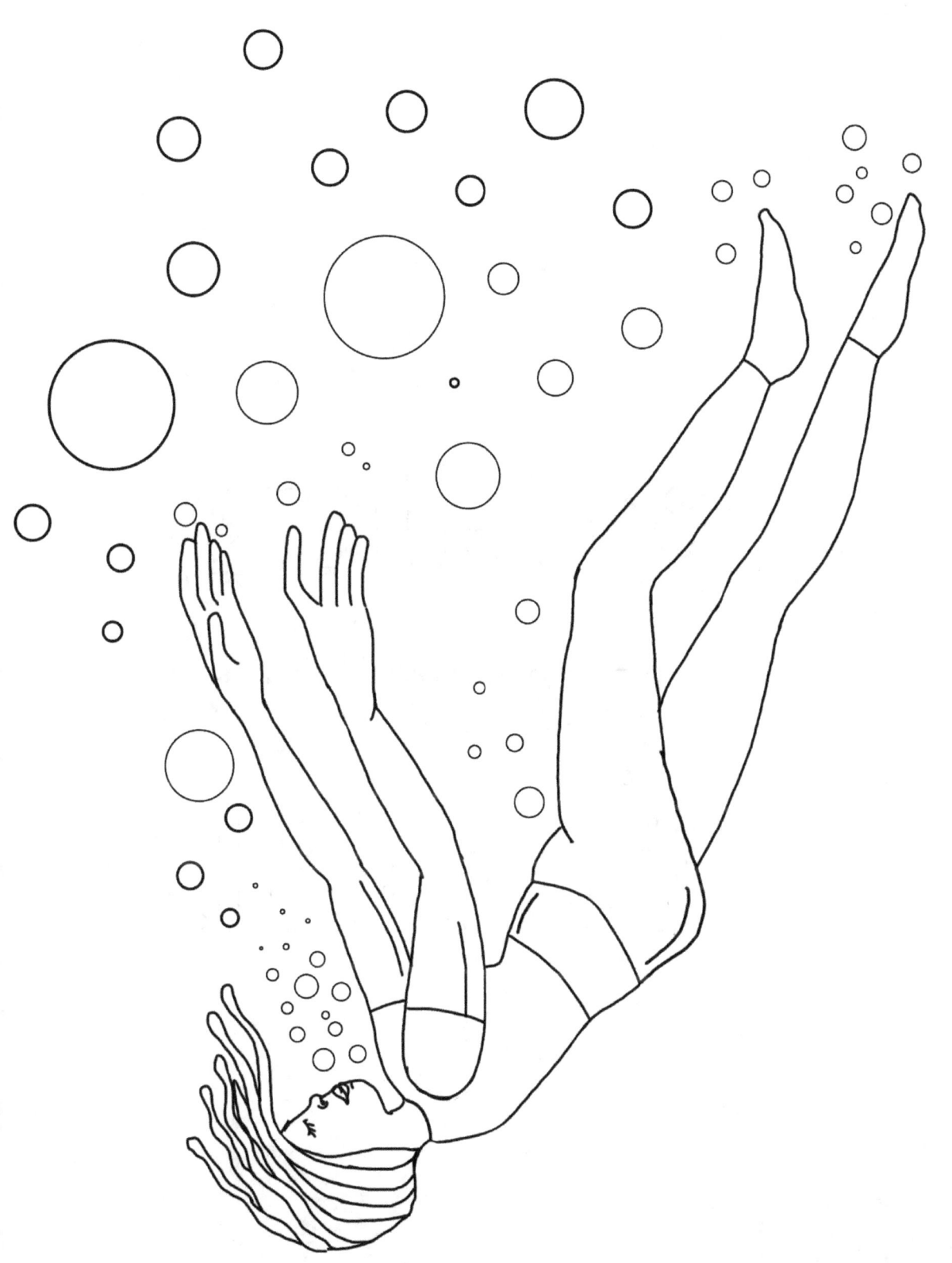

I bring something special to this world.

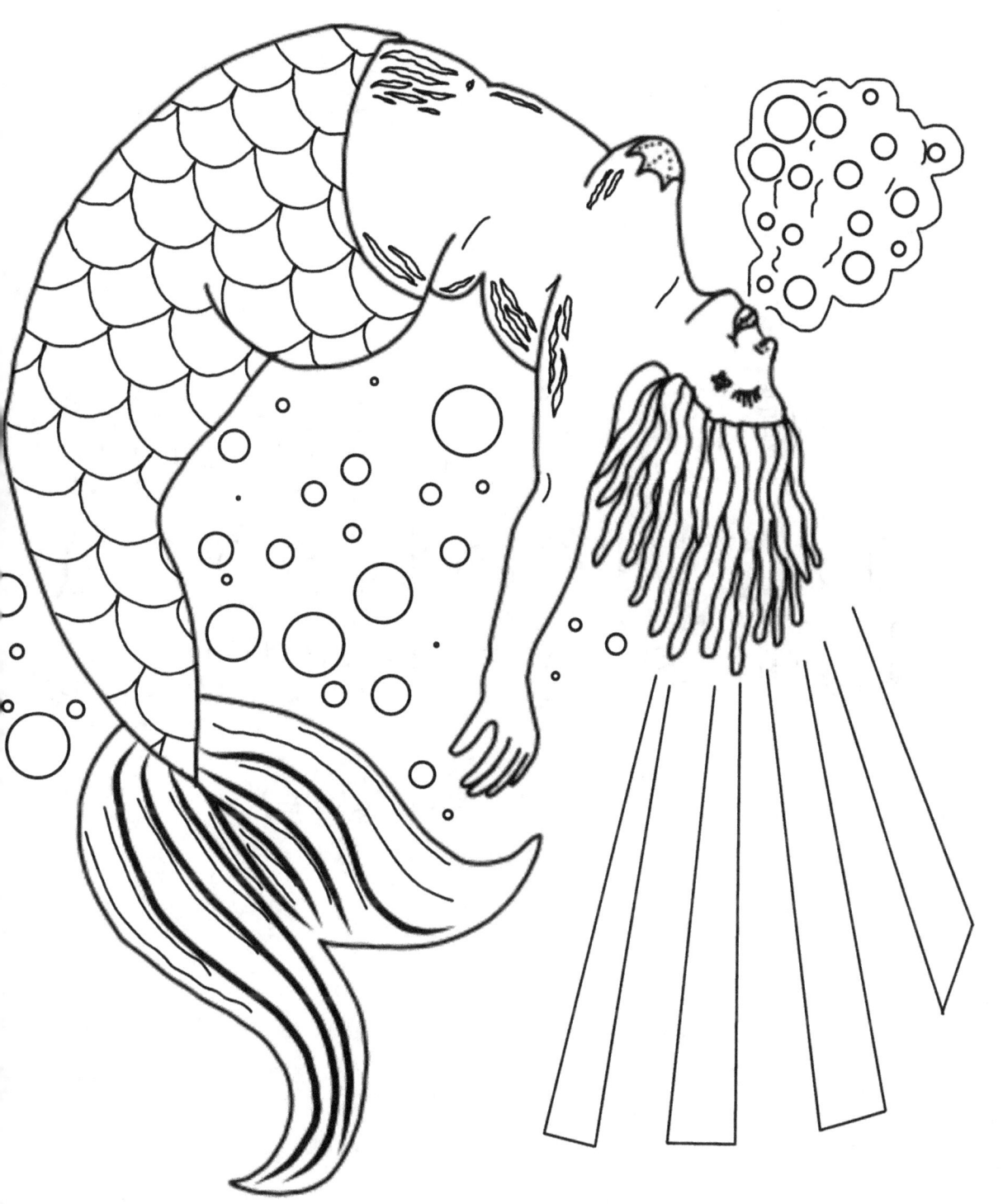

If my strength intimidates you, that's a weakness of yours.

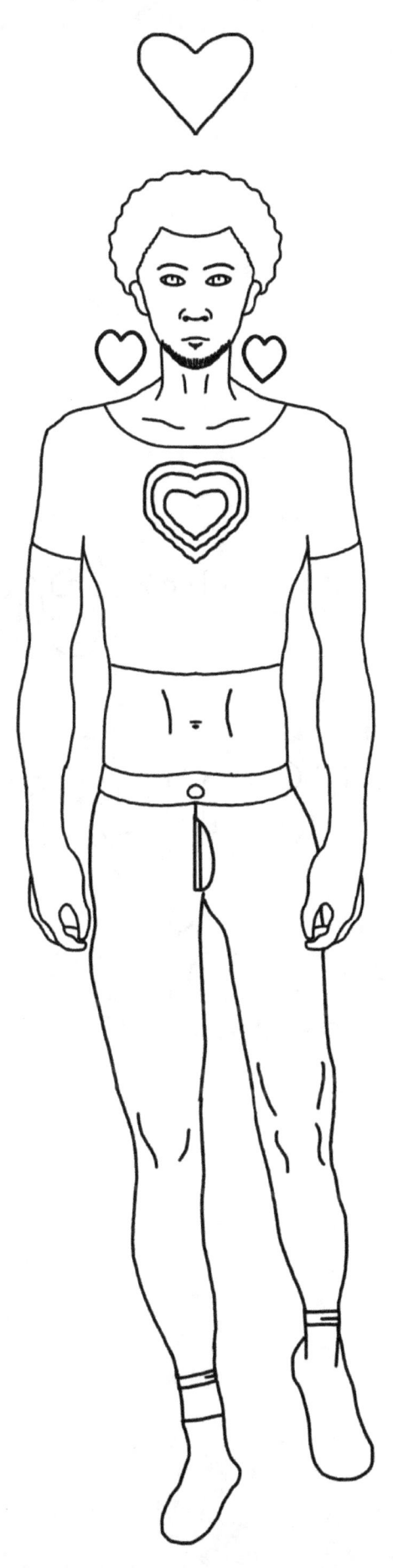

Change is scary, not changing is scarier.

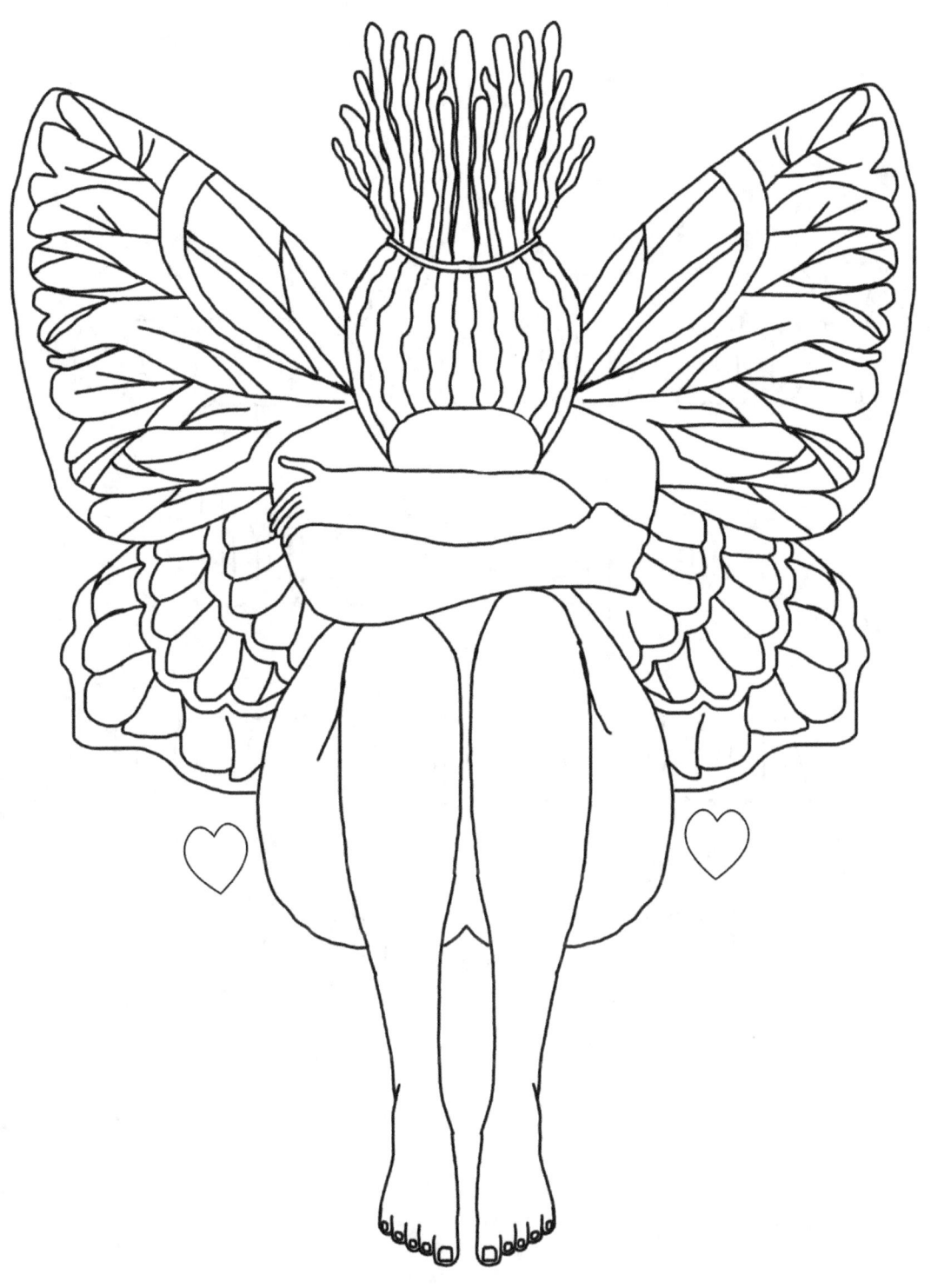

You don't have to pretend you're okay if you're not.

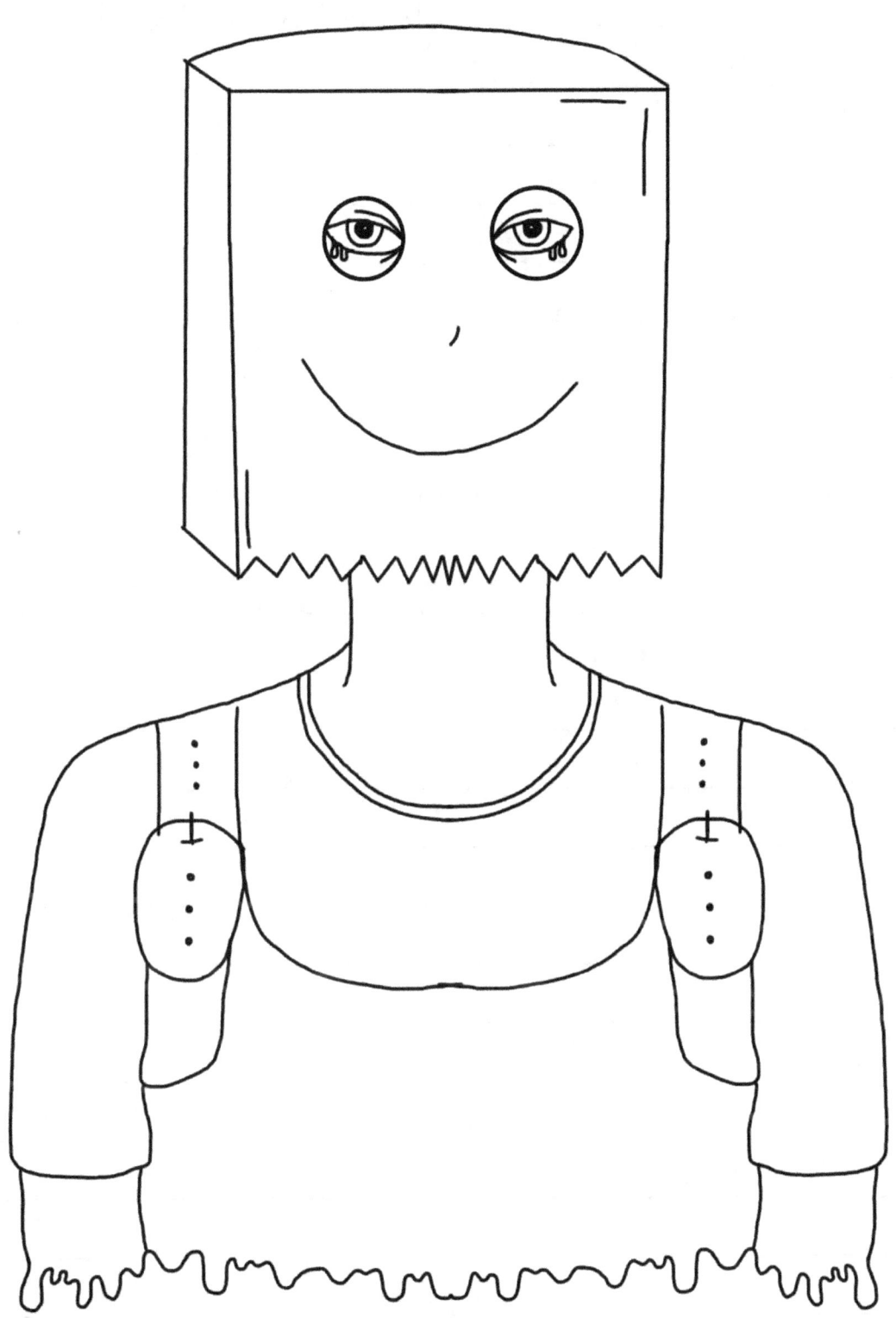

Positive Affirmations.

Write down the positive ways you've changed in the past 5 years.

I choose to let go of the pain in my past and anxiety about my future.

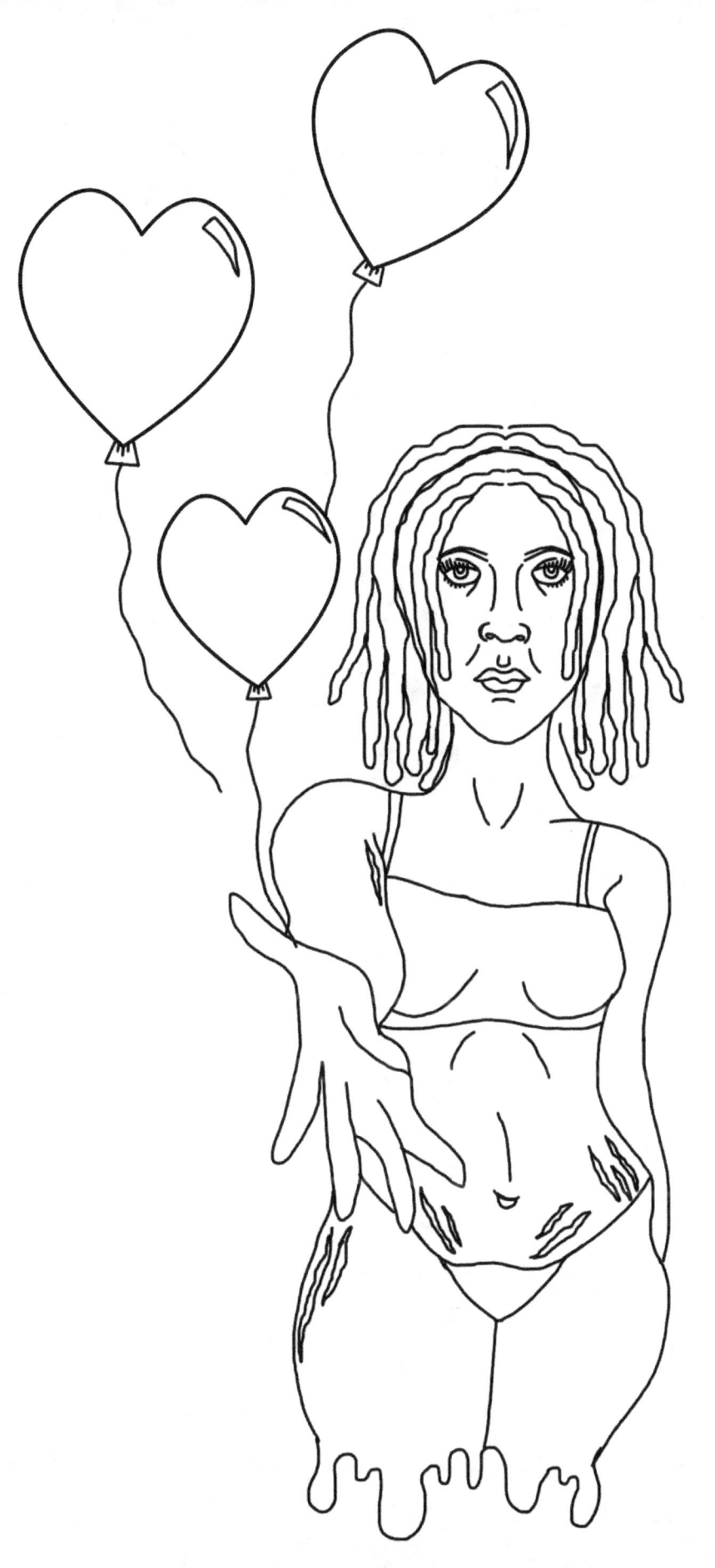

A Safe Place To Vent:

www.ingramcontent.com/pod-product-compliance
Lightning Source LLC
Chambersburg PA
CBHW081708220526
45466CB00009B/2918